# The Raja's Elephants

## by Amber Waverly
## illustrated by Alex De Lange

**Harcourt**

Orlando   Boston   Dallas   Chicago   San Diego

Visit *The Learning Site!*
**www.harcourtschool.com**

Years ago, there was none of the machinery that we take for granted today. Jobs that required heavy lifting were not done with cranes. How was the work done, then? In what are now India, Pakistan, and Bangladesh, the work was done with the help of elephants.

Elephants have actually been used as servants for thousands of years. Four thousand years ago, in what is now Pakistan, there was a famous city called Mohenjo-Daro. When some archaeologists discovered the ruins of that city,

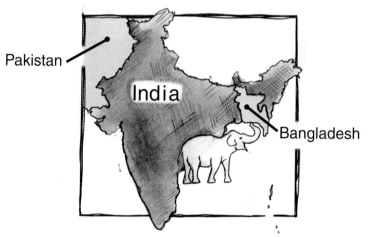

they found stones with pictures of elephants carved on them. The elephants seemed to be wearing cloths or saddles on their backs. This could mean that 4,000 years ago, elephants were already being tamed and trained.

Hundreds of years ago, each of India's many provinces was ruled by a person known as a *raja*. The *raja* was a wealthy prince. Among his most prized possessions were his elephants.

The *rajas* used their elephants to haul great blocks of stone. The stones were used to build palaces and temples. The elephants were also used to haul trees and logs and to plow fields. Later, when machines became available, it was no longer necessary to use elephants to help with heavy lifting. However, elephants are still used to haul logs in places where there is no heavy machinery.

In 326 B.C., King Porus of India used 200 elephants in a battle against the invading armies of Alexander the Great. This was the first recorded use of elephants in a war. The elephants wore platforms on their backs where soldiers sat and threw spears at the enemy. These platforms or towers were known as castles. In later years, Indians protected the heads and chests of their war elephants with armor.

Unfortunately, *raja*s often went to war against neighboring provinces. In the early 1600s, a powerful *raja* conquered much of India. Known as the Great Mogul, he owned huge herds of elephants. He not only owned a great many work elephants, but he also kept 300 elephants to ride. He had 40,000 more elephants available to lead into battle. Today, elephants still take part in traditional military ceremonies in India.

The *rajas* also used their elephants in peacetime activities. These included royal weddings, state ceremonies, and religious processions. On special occasions, the elephants would be bathed in pure water. Then they were sprinkled with perfumes. An artist would paint designs on their heads and ears in bright colors. The elephant's tusks would be scrubbed clean and decorated with gold paint. A fancy cloak of red, gold, purple, and yellow would be draped over each elephant's back. Then the elephant was ready to be paraded in public for all to admire. Several people rode in an elaborate wooden seat called a *howdah*. It was strapped to the elephant's back.

Elephants were usually treated very well by the *rajas*. The elephants helped the *rajas* be successful. Elephants made it easier for them to build things and to develop and protect their land. A *raja* with many elephants was considered to be very powerful.

Many *rajas* valued their elephants so highly that they implored their subjects to treat the animals well. Anyone who killed an elephant would be punished severely.

*Rajas* made sure that their elephants were fed plentifully. During times of drought, only a trickle of rain would fall. The water in rivers and streams would become very shallow. Crops would die, and the result would be a famine. Poor peasants and people in the villages would go hungry. Even then, the elephants would be fed plentifully from the *raja's* storehouse.

The *rajas* employed people to care for and train their elephants. Professional elephant trainers were known as *mahouts*. They worked with wild elephants that had been captured, as well as with those born in captivity. A *mahout* learned his skills from his father and passed them on to his sons. His sons, in turn, would pass along their skills to their sons.

Before wild elephants could be trained, they had to be captured. The most widely used method was to herd the elephants into a corral, known as a *keddah*. Men called beaters made a lot of noise behind the elephants. They beat on pans, shook rattles, and screamed. The frightened animals moved away from the beaters and right into the *keddah*. After they were trapped behind the closed gate, trainers chose the elephants they thought they could train.

An elephant usually made friends with only one person at a time. That person is the only one the elephant would obey. A *mahout* would spend many years working with the same elephant. Some *mahouts* felt that elephants should be taught only with kindness. Others believed that the best training combined reward and punishment. All *mahouts* agreed that during training, an elephant must never be allowed to disobey a single command. With courage, patience, and kindness, *mahouts* won the respect of their elephants.

The days of the *rajas* have long since passed. The role of elephants in India is very different from what it once was. Still, *mahouts* in India and other places in Southeast Asia train elephants for hauling logs. Elephants participate in ceremonies in India. Some *mahouts* take tourists for rides on their elephants. The 4,000-year-old tradition of working with elephants continues.

## Indian and African Elephants

Indian elephants and African elephants have several different characteristics. Indian elephants are smaller and have smaller tusks. They also have lighter skin, and their ears are only half as large as those of African elephants. In addition, their backs arch up. African elephants' backs dip down.

**African Elephant**

**Indian Elephant**

However, these two kinds of elephants are similar in many ways. Both Indian and African elephants cool themselves by flapping their ears. They also use their long trunks to spray themselves with water. Finally, they all roll in mud. The mud stays on their skin and blocks the burning rays of the sun.

Next time you see an elephant, try to figure out whether it is an Indian elephant or an African elephant!